# Living Radically

Jordan Whittington

# Contents

# About the Author

Jordan Whittington is the College Pastor at First Baptist Church of College Station where he daily has the opportunity to pour into the lives of college students at Texas A&M University and Blinn College. Jordan is married to Carlin, who teaches 3rd Grade, and they have one son, Cooper. Jordan is a proud graduate of The University of Alabama (Roll Tide) as well as Beeson Divinity School (Soli Deo Gloria).

# An Introduction to Living Radically

**Purpose:**
Welcome to Live Radically, a study through the book of 1 Peter. This book is intended to guide small group discussion, to help members to have a more thorough understanding of 1 Peter, and to encourage real life application of the scriptures. Each lesson has scripture to read (printed in the book to encourage annotations) and questions related to the text. Each member of the group should have a copy of this book so they can read the scriptures and answer the questions each week before meeting. My hope is that this book is a helpful resource for you and your group as you seek to Live Radically.

**Sections:**
**Read the Word:**
Each lesson starts with the scripture for the week. The purpose is to take time to read and understand the message, context, and purpose of the text. So, read it as many times as you need in order to understand what you are reading. Take time to mark up the text with notes, highlights, or even questions you have about the reading.

**Examine the Word:** After you have read through the text, it is time to interact with it. In this section, you will be prompted to write your "One Big Thing", "One Confusing Thing", and "One Way I Must Respond." These three prompts are intended to help you consider the big picture of what you read. What stands out? What doesn't make sense? How does this apply?

Next, you will be prompted to consider a few questions. These questions are intended to make you think critically about the text. Take time to think through thorough and complete answers to the questions. Allow time to really think through your answers even if you think of an answer immediately. Make sure you write down your responses as a way to help you think and so you remember your thoughts during discussion.

**Notes:** Each text will have footnotes and other related verses to consider. These notes are meant to help you understand the scripture better and make connections to other texts. The goal of the notes is to assist in personal study, not to be an answer key. As you study the text, the notes will give you further insight to the language, context, and concepts of the text. The related verses should support the message of 1 Peter and allow you to see how it relates to the rest of the Bible.

**Discussion:** When you come together as a group, read the text together and discuss the questions. The questions are not meant to give strict order to the discussion, but they are a great starting point. I encourage you to share what you have learned, but go to your discussion with the primary goal of learning from the other members of your group.

Special thanks to Aaron Macias for his vision, creativity, and willingness to create cover art for each of our bible studies.

Special thanks to Asher Ardizzoni for his help developing questions and editing the out all of my grammatical, syntactical, and spelling errors.

# Overview of 1 Peter

LESSON 1

## Lesson 1 – An Overview

### Introduction and Purpose of the 1 Peter

Peter, the bold and sometimes brash, disciple of Jesus is writing to men and women who have been exiled due to persecution for their faith. Peter, who is likely writing this from prison, understands this testing first-hand. Peter's purpose is brought to light in his final words (5:12) where he states that this letter is the "true grace of God" written to encourage the recipients to "stand firm."

Peter's letter can be difficult to digest as it reveals that following Jesus does not lead to a simple, and problem free life. The suffering of Peter's audience could end if only they would denounce their faith in Jesus Christ. Yet, Peter not only exhorts his readers to "stand firm," he also calls them to new heights of holy living. The letter studied in this book is truly a call to live radically.

### Audience

While most of Paul's letters are directed at a specific church or person, Peter is writing to a group of people spread out of a land mass nearly the size of the state of California.[1] As a result, this letter does not focus on specific concerns, but rather, more general issues, making it applicable to a wide-range of recipients. Peter knows first-hand what they have experienced, and history will show that the persecution will only intensify for the next 100 years. Peter encourages his audience to look past the immediate trial and to hold fast to the "living hope" (1:3) that is found in Jesus Christ.

**Read the entire book of 1 Peter** (roughly a 20-minute read).

As you read, consider what subjects are being repeated, what ideas are being built upon, and what you believe Peter is trying to convey in his writing.

After reading, consider the following questions:
What section(s) of the book was most impactful for you? Why?

From your reading, what main points do you believe Peter is wanting his audience to remember?

---

[1] Jobes, Karen, 1 Peter, Baker Exegetical Commentary on the New Testament, 19.

Which section(s) of the book left you confused or in need of more information?

As we study the book of 1 Peter, what area do you hope to grow in personally?

What do you hope to receive from this group?

**Why Living Radically?**
Peter is calling people to do what only makes sense if God is truly God, if Jesus is truly our savior, and if the Spirit is truly dwelling in us. To people experiencing great suffering and persecution, Peter calls for deeper devotion to God. Peter examines every facet of life and excepts nothing less than radical and complete commitment to godliness. The call to radical living does not end with Christianity becoming comfortable or mainstream. We must listen closely to the words of Peter. We must respond in faith. We must live radically.

Take time to pray in response to what you have read and for your study of the book of 1 Peter.

# A Living Hope in a Dying World

## LESSON 2

# A Living Hope in a Dying World
1 Peter 1:1-7 Christian Standard Bible [CSB]

Peter, an apostle of Jesus Christ:

To those chosen[1], living as exiles[2] dispersed abroad in Pontus, Galatia, Cappadocia, Asia, and Bithynia, chosen [2] according to the foreknowledge of God the Father, through the sanctifying work of the Spirit, to be obedient and to be sprinkled with the blood of Jesus Christ.[3]

May grace and peace be multiplied to you.

[3] Blessed be the God and Father of our Lord Jesus Christ. Because of his great mercy he has given us new birth into a living hope[4] through the resurrection of Jesus Christ from the dead [4] and into an inheritance[5] that is imperishable, undefiled, and unfading,[6] kept in heaven for you. [5] You are being guarded by God's power through faith[7] for a salvation that is ready to be revealed in the last time. [6] You rejoice in this, even though now for a short time, if necessary, you suffer grief in various trials[8] [7] so that the proven character of your faith— more valuable than gold[9] which, though perishable, is refined by fire—may result in praise, glory, and honor at the revelation of Jesus Christ.

One Big Thing:

One Confusing Thing:

---

[1] In the Old Testament, Israel was often referred to as God's chosen people. Now, in the New Testament, the chosen people are not tied to a birth lineage but to those who have been born again through faith in Jesus Christ. This includes the Jews and the Gentiles as the chosen people of God.

[2] Exile is the removal from your home which also brings about loss of certain rights and privileges (Jobes, 1 Peter, 61). Christians were despised by the Romans. Under the reign of Nero, Christians are blamed for the burning of Rome (John MacArthur, The MacArthur Bible Commentary, 1900).

[3] Peter is bringing out a trinitarian perspective both to the believer's salvation as well as suffering. God is not surprised by the situation but is instead using this experience to sanctify his people.

[4] A living hope is especially powerful to a people fearing death. "Whatever happens to them in this world is trivial compared to the blessing of the future resurrection" (Thomas Schreiner, 1,2 Peter, Jude, The New American Commentary, 62).

[5] Peter reminds his hearers that have potentially lost everything (finances, family, security) for the sake of Christ that an inheritance awaits them, which in fact is being guarded (v5) by God himself.

[6] The promised inheritance will not lose any value or beauty. This contrasts well with Jesus' teaching on earthly wealth which "moths and rust destroy" (Matthew 6:19-21).

[7] For Peter, faith is a constant and continual trust in God, not a single act or event (Schreiner, 1,2 Peter, Jude, 64).

[8] Trials are temptations of faith as "no genuine faith will exist without [trials]" (Jobes, 1 Peter, 87).

[9] Fire is used to test the genuineness of gold. Peter uses this analogy to connect suffering as the test of a believer's faith. True faith can withstand the fire.

Why would God choose these people yet allow them to be exiled?

While we don't fear exile, what trial are you most fearful of?

How do you think your faith would look different if you experienced persecution for their faith?

How do you understand the term living hope? How can you live that out?

Sanctification is the "progressive growth of holiness." In what ways is God sanctifying you currently?

Reread verses 6-7. How can you respond with praise, glory, and honor?

What makes this passage radical?

One Way I Must Respond:

Scriptures to consider:
Matthew 6:19-21
2 Corinthians 11:24-28
James 1:12

# Faith in the Unseen

LESSON 3

## <u>Faith in the Unseen</u>
1 Peter 1:8-12 [CSB]

[8] Though you have not seen him,[1] you love him; though not seeing him now, you believe in him, and you rejoice with inexpressible and glorious joy, [9] because you are receiving the goal of your faith, the salvation of your souls.[2]

[10] Concerning this salvation, the prophets,[3] who prophesied about the grace that would come to you, searched and carefully investigated. [11] They inquired into what time or what circumstances the Spirit of Christ within them was indicating when he testified in advance to the sufferings of Christ and the glories that would follow.[a] [12] It was revealed to them that they were not serving themselves but you. These things have now been announced to you[4] through those who preached the gospel to you by the Holy Spirit sent from heaven—angels long to catch a glimpse of these things.[5]

One Big Thing:

One Confusing Thing:

---

[1] Peter is writing to followers of Jesus who like you and me have never seen the historical Jesus in the flesh (Schreiner, 1,2 Peter, Jude, 69) and yet still love him.

[2] Verse 9 clarifies that the love and joy experienced now is rooted in the hope for the completion of salvation and entrance into Heaven (Ibid., 70).

[3] Peter is referencing the Old Testament prophets who both foretold of the coming Messiah, but also studied carefully previous prophesies to more fully understand the work God was going to do in our world (Ibid., 72).

[4] While they have not seen Christ in the flesh, they are blessed to live in a day when the work of Christ has been revealed and is more fully understood (Jobes, 1 Peter, 97).

[5] Peter encourages "his readers, who were suffering a loss of status in their society because of Christ, that in fact they were more privileged" in understanding the work of God through Christ than the Old Testament prophets and even the angels (Ibid,, 104).

Is faith in Jesus Christ blind faith? Explain.

Why does God require faith instead of giving "definitive proof"?

How does a Christian rejoice in what is not seen?

What circumstances in your life or aspects of the Christian faith have caused you to doubt?

How have you dealt with these doubts? Have you ever shared your doubts?

Is it wrong to doubt?

Is your faith marked by inexpressible and glorious joy? What needs to happen for that to be a reality?

What makes this passage radical?

One Way I Must Respond:

Verses to consider:
Hebrews 11:1
John 20:24-29
Mark 9:20-24

# A Radical Call

LESSON 4

# <u>Lesson 4 – A Radical Call</u>
1 Peter 1:13-25 (CSB)

[13] Therefore,[1] with your minds ready for action, be sober-minded[2] and set your hope completely on the grace[3] to be brought to you at the revelation of Jesus Christ. [14] As obedient children, do not be conformed to the desires of your former ignorance. [15] But as the one who called you is holy, you also are to be holy in all your conduct;[4] [16] for it is written, **Be holy,[5] because I am holy.**

[17] If you appeal to the Father who judges impartially according to each one's work,[6] you are to conduct yourselves in reverence during your time living as strangers.[7] [18] For you know that you were redeemed from your empty way of life inherited from your ancestors, not with perishable things like silver or gold, [19] but with the precious blood of Christ, like that of an unblemished and spotless lamb.[8] [20] He was foreknown before the foundation of the world but was revealed in these last times for you. [21] Through him you believe in God, who raised him from the dead and gave him glory, so that your faith and hope are in God.

[22] Since you have purified yourselves by your obedience to the truth, so that you show sincere brotherly love for each other, from a pure heart love one another constantly, [23] because you have been born again—not of perishable seed but of imperishable—through the living and enduring word of God.[9] [24] For

**All flesh is like grass, and all its glory like a flower of the grass.**
**The grass withers, and the flower falls, [25] but the word of the Lord endures forever.[10]**
And this word is the gospel that was proclaimed to you.

---

[1] The call to action that follows is rooted in the living hope and sure faith of 1 Peter 1:8-9. Faith is a prerequisite to faithful obedience. All imperatives of "Christian living" come on the heels of what God has already done (Jobes, 1 Peter, 109).

[2] Or Self-controlled (New International Version [NIV]). The call to holy living "requires effort, concentration, and intentionality" (Schreiner, 1, 2 Peter, Jude, 78).

[3] "God's commands are always rooted in his grace" (Ibid., 77).

[4] "The call is to live differently, not just practice religion differently" (Jobes, 1 Peter, 113). Every facet of life must be different.

[5] To be holy is to be perfect in goodness and righteousness.

[6] The one who appeals to the Father as judge most basically is understood to be a Christian (MacArthur, The MacArthur Bible Commentary, 1906). As a result, any Christian is then urged to live in reverence to God.

[7] The concept of "stranger" can apply to today as biblical Christianity is strange not only to non-believers but even those who consider themselves Christians.

[8] Peter is connecting Jesus to the perfect sacrifice of the Old Testament which was required to be without blemish or spot. (Exodus 29:1, Leviticus 1:3).

[9] The call for Christians to love is rooted in the "first love" (1 John 4:10-11)

[10] Isaiah 40:6. Peter is reminding the people of God of the power of God even while the powers of the world are afflicting them.

One Big Thing:

One Confusing Thing:

What are the desires of former ignorance Peter is referring to?

How would you explain the concept and meaning of holy to a non-believer?

How does holy living differ from the typical (cultural) Christianity most commonly taught/seen?

Is faithfulness to the word of God a requirement for keeping salvation? Explain your answer.

Why should a Christian live holy?

What are the costs of holy living?

What are the benefits of holy living?

What aspect of your life conflicts with holiness?

What makes this passage radical?


One way I must respond:


Scripture to Consider:
Ephesians 4:17-24
Romans 6:1-2
1 John 4:7-11

# A Radical People

LESSON 5

# A Radical People

1 Peter 2:1-12 (ESV)

So put away all malice and all deceit and hypocrisy and envy and all slander. [2] Like newborn infants, long for the pure spiritual milk,[1] that by it you may grow up into salvation— [3] if[2] indeed you have tasted that the Lord is good.

[4] As you come to him, a living stone rejected by men but in the sight of God chosen and precious, [5] you yourselves like living stones are being built up as a spiritual house, to be a holy priesthood, to offer spiritual sacrifices acceptable to God through Jesus Christ. [6] For it stands in Scripture:

"Behold, I am laying in Zion a stone,
    a cornerstone[3] chosen and precious,
and whoever believes in him will not be put to shame."[4]

[7] So the honor is for you who believe, but for those who do not believe,
"The stone that the builders rejected[5] has become the cornerstone,"

[8] and "A stone of stumbling,  and a rock of offense."[6] They stumble because they disobey the word, as they were destined[7] to do.

[9] But you are a chosen race, a royal priesthood,[8] a holy nation, a people for his own possession, that you may proclaim[9] the excellencies of him who called you out of

---

[1] "Peter sees milk as that which all Christians need in order to nurture their new life in Christ, so that they will 'grow up' into salvation" (Jobes, 1 Peter, 132). The reference to milk should not be seen as immaturity (as is used in 1 Corinthians 3:1-3 and Hebrews 5:11-14) but is for all who seek to live in godliness and holiness (Schreiner, 1, 2 Peter, Jude, 99).

[2] While Peter does not question whether his audience has experienced the goodness of God, the use of "if" causes the people to contemplate the work of God on their behalf (Ibid., 101).

[3] Jesus Christ is the sure, foundation piece in the life of a believer.

[4] Isaiah 28:16. Peter understands the life of a Christian follows the pattern of Jesus: Rejected by men yet chosen by God (Ibid., 104).

[5] Christians endured "verbal abuse designed to demean, discredit, and shame the believers as social deviants and moral deviants endangering the common good (Jobes, 1 Peter, 152).

[6] MacArthur notes "Christ is either the means of salvation" to those who believe or "the means of judgment" to those who reject him.

[7] The issue of God's sovereignty and man's responsibility is brought to the forefront. Schreiner argues that while "God ordains all things", humans are still responsible for their choices. God does not coerce people against their will to sin (Schreiner, 1, 2 Peter, Jude, 113).

[8] The purpose of the priest was to mediate between God and his people. Christians are now deemed priests who can approach God personally as well as for the sake of those around them.

[9] The glorious designations given to Christians comes with a clear mission, namely, to proclaim the Gospel of God to the world. The word "proclaim", found nowhere else in the New Testament, means to "tell something not otherwise known" (John MacArthur, The MacArthur Biblical Commentary, 1909).

darkness into his marvelous light. [10] Once you were not a people, but now you are God's people; once you had not received mercy, but now you have received mercy.

[11] Beloved, I urge you as sojourners and exiles[10] to abstain from the passions of the flesh, which wage war against your soul. [12] Keep your conduct among the Gentiles honorable, so that when they speak against you as evildoers, they may see your good deeds and glorify God on the day of visitation.

One Big Thing:

One Confusing Thing:

What is required to "taste that the Lord is good"? Have you experienced this?

In verse 4, Peter understands us to be chose and precious in the eyes of God. How does your opinion of yourself differ from God's opinion of yourself? Which is correct?

Peter uses three Old Testament quotations referencing Jesus as the "cornerstone". Pick one of the three and briefly explain how Jesus fulfills this prophecy.

------

[10] Though Peter's audience is under constant scrutiny and persecution, how they live among unbelievers can have kingdom impact. Exile does not eliminate influence.

What makes a person a part of God's "chosen race, royal priesthood… people of his own possession"?

What does it mean to grow up into salvation?

Read 2:11-12 again. Practically, how does the way you live point others to Christ? Have you ever seen fruit from this?

What makes this passage radical?

One Way I Must Respond:

Scriptures to Consider:
Psalm 34: 1-8
Ephesians 2:11-22
Romans 9:14-26

# Radical Submission

LESSON 6

# **Radical Submission**

1 Peter 2:13-25  (CSB)

[13] Submit to every human authority because of the Lord[1], whether to the emperor as the supreme authority [14] or to governors as those sent out by him to punish those who do what is evil and to praise those who do what is good. [15] For it is God's will that you silence the ignorance of foolish people by doing good. [16] Submit as free[2] people, not using your freedom as a cover-up for evil, but as God's slaves.[3] [17] Honor everyone. Love the brothers and sisters. Fear God.[4] Honor the emperor.

[18] Household slaves, submit to your masters with all reverence not only to the good and gentle ones but also to the cruel.[5] [19] For it brings favor if, because of a consciousness of God, someone endures grief from suffering unjustly.[6] [20] For what credit is there if when you do wrong and are beaten, you endure it? But when you do what is good and suffer, if you endure it, this brings favor with God.

[21] For you were called to this, because Christ also suffered for you, leaving you an example, that you should follow in his steps. [22] He did not commit sin, **and no deceit was found in his mouth;** [23] when he was insulted, he did not insult in return; when he suffered, he did not threaten but entrusted himself to the one who judges justly. [24] He himself bore our sins in his body on the tree; so that, having died to sins, we might live for righteousness. **By his wounds you have been healed.**[7] [25] For you **were like sheep going astray,** but you have now returned to the Shepherd and Overseer of your souls.

---

[1] Clearly, Peter understands that God, not the emperor, is the supreme authority ruling in the world (Schreiner, 1, 2 Peter, Jude, 126).

[2] True freedom is doing what is good. A life that abuses freedom for evil is a life still enslaved by sin (Ibid., 131).

[3] Paul understands a life as a Christian to be a life enslaved to Christ (Romans 6:15-23). "One is either a slave of sin or a slave to God" (Ibid., 131).

[4] "Christian freedom rests not on escape from service but on a change of master" (Jobes, 1 Peter, 177). In serving God, every facet of life (social, spiritual, political) ought to be honor God.

[5] Peter is calling for submission even to unfair and harsh masters (MacArthur, The MacArthur Biblical Commentary, 1910).

[6] Favor is found when even in the midst of unfair treatment, a servant [employee] clings to God's "sovereign care rather than responding in anger, hostility, discontent, pride or rebellion (Ibid., 1911)

[7] While our suffering can lead others to an understanding of the gospel (2:12), our suffering does not complete the same work as that of Jesus Christ's. Jesus, by his sinless life and obedient death, is the only one who could bear our sins.

One Big Thing:

One Confusing Thing:

In your own words, define submission.

When, if ever, is it right to rebel against an authority?

How can you honor a leader with whom you disagree?

What does it mean to "submit as free people"?

In what way is your submission incomplete?

Do you consider yourself a slave to Christ? Why or why not?

What is God's favor?

Have you ever done anything in obedience to God that has led to rejection? Explain.

Why does God allow ungodly leaders?

What makes this passage radical?

One Way I Must Respond:

Scriptures to Consider:
Romans 13:1-5
Jeremiah 29:7
Titus 3:1-2
Colossians 3:22-25
Mark 12:14-17

# A Radical Marriage

LESSON 7

## __Radical Marriage__
1 Peter 3:1-7 (CSB)


In the same way, wives,[1] submit[2] yourselves to your own[3] husbands so that, even if some disobey the word, they may be won over without a word by the way their wives live [2] when they observe your pure, reverent lives. [3] Don't let your beauty consist of outward things like elaborate hairstyles and wearing gold jewelry or fine clothes,[4] [4] but rather what is inside the heart—the imperishable quality of a gentle and quiet spirit, which is of great worth in God's sight. [5] For in the past, the holy women who put their hope in God also adorned themselves in this way, submitting to their own husbands, [6] just as Sarah obeyed Abraham, calling him lord. You have become her children when you do what is good and do not fear any intimidation.[5]

[7] Husbands, in the same way, live with your wives in an understanding way, as with a weaker partner,[6] showing them honor as coheirs[7] of the grace of life, so that your prayers will not be hindered.

---

[1] As in lesson 6, Peter focuses his words on the relational partner with less power (first slaves, now wives). These vulnerable roles are representative of the church Peter is writing to in many ways (Schreiner, 1, 2 Peter, Jude, 148).

[2] Once again, this is voluntary submission, not forced upon the woman (Schreiner, 1, 2 Peter, Jude, 148). In Ephesians 5:22-33, Paul shows that marital submission is a picture of the church's submission to Christ's authority. Christ as the loving "husband" never abuses his bride or her submission.

[3] Peter is clear that the submission of the wife is only to her husband. No other man has authority to determine a woman's role or rights beyond her husband and governing authority (Jobes, 1 Peter, 203). Simply by addressing the slave and wife, Peter is ascribing value and responsibility which was uncommon in Greek culture (Ibid., 204).

[4] The "outward things" were often thought to be attempts to seduce or deceive men. To adorn such things in worship, especially if the husband was not a believer nor in attendance, would call into question the woman's intentions (Ibid., 205). By not partaking in outward beauty practices, the intention of the wife would be clear: to worship her God (Ibid., 205).

[5] Peter understand that believing wives will not always behave in a way that pleases their husbands because at times their loyalty to God will transcend their duty to submit to husbands. In such cases they are not to fear but hope in God…" (Schreiner, 1, 2 Peter, Jude, 158).

[6] Women are not weaker intellectually, emotionally, morally, or spiritually. Peter must be referring to anatomical strength – "sheer strength" (Ibid., 160). Peter's usage of "weaker partner" can be a way to indirectly speak against physical abuse or any ungodly wielding of power over a woman that society may allow (Jobes, 1 Peter, 209).

[7] Be careful not to focus solely on "weaker partner" and miss that women are coheirs with men of the same grace and promise through Jesus Christ. God shows no partiality (Romans 2:11).

One Big Thing:

One Confusing Thing:

Hoes does the text "wives submit to your husband" make you feel?

How does your initial interpretation differ from what Peter is saying?

What about this view of marriage would our society struggle to accept? What about this view of marriage do you still struggle to accept?

In what situation(s) should a wife not submit to her husband?

Is it right to marry an unbeliever?

As believers, how can we live in line with verse 3 appropriately?

Does this passage portray men and women as unequal? How would you explain this to a non-believer?

What do we sacrifice if we do not accept Peter's view of marriage?

What makes this passage radical?

Scriptures to Consider:
Ephesians 5:22-33
Proverbs 31:30

# Radical Suffering

## LESSON 8

# **Radical Suffering**

1 Peter 3:8-22 English Standard Version (ESV)

[8] Finally, all of you,[1] have unity of mind, sympathy, brotherly[2] love, a tender heart, and a humble mind. [9] Do not repay evil for evil or reviling for reviling, but on the contrary, bless[3], for to this you were called, that you may obtain a blessing. [10] For

"Whoever desires to love life
   and see good days,
let him keep his tongue from evil
   and his lips from speaking deceit;
[11] let him turn away from evil and do good;
   let him seek peace and pursue it.
[12] For the eyes of the Lord are on the righteous,
   and his ears are open to their prayer.
But the face of the Lord is against those who do evil."[4]


[13] Now who is there to harm you if you are zealous for what is good? [14] But even if you should suffer for righteousness' sake, you will be blessed. Have no fear of them, nor be troubled, [15] but in your hearts honor Christ the Lord as holy, always being prepared to make a defense to anyone who asks you[5] for a reason for the hope that is in you; yet do it with gentleness and respect, [16] having a good conscience, so that, when you are slandered, those who revile your good behavior in Christ may be put to shame. [17] For it is better to suffer for doing good, if that should be God's will,[6] than for doing evil.

[18] For Christ also suffered once for sins, the righteous for the unrighteous, that he might bring us to God, being put to death in the flesh but made alive in the spirit, [19] in which he went and proclaimed to the spirits in prison, [20] because they formerly did not obey, when

---

[1] Peter has spent time specifically speaking to certain members of the congregation (slaves, wives, and husbands) but the godly traits exhorted in 3:8 are for all believers. No one is exempt.

[2] Peter is calling the people to love one another the same way they would love a family member (Jobes, 1 Peter, 214).

[3] This word carried the meaning of "publicly speak[ing] well of someone" (Jobes 218). Schreiner understands this to mean "ask[ing] God to show his favor and grace" on the one causing harm (Schreiner, 1, 2 Peter, Jude, 164-5).

[4] Peter is not demanding a perfect life in order to receive God's favor, but Peter does believe that a life changed by Jesus Christ will live differently (Ibid., 168). "Changed lives live changed lives".

[5] To make a defense is to explain and share what you believe and why you believe to someone who is asking. This is not an argumentative discussion (Ibid., 174). The expectation is not for every believer to be an expert, but that every believer should know the essentials of Christianity and be able to share this with someone who is interested.

[6] Peter understands suffering can be a part of God's will. While suffering varies upon each believer, the suffering endured is under God's control (Ibid., 179).

God's patience waited in the days of Noah,[7] while the ark was being prepared, in which a few, that is, eight persons, were brought safely through water. [21] Baptism, which corresponds to this, now saves you, not as a removal of dirt from the body but as an appeal to God for a good conscience, through the resurrection of Jesus Christ, [22] who has gone into heaven and is at the right hand of God, with angels, authorities, and powers having been subjected to him

One Big Thing:

One Confusing Thing:

What hope is Peter sharing by quoting from Psalm 34:12-16 in verses 10-12?

What is in mind when Peter says "make a defense"? Do you feel prepared to make a defense?

Why does attitude matter when making a defense?

---

[7] Peter uses Noah's story to encourage his audience that history has shown how the majority culture has rejected God, yet God remained faithful to his people and saved them. The suffering Christians can find hope in Noah's obedience as they strive to remain obedient each day.

How would you explain 3:13 and 3:17 to someone new to Christianity or who is considering faith in Jesus Christ?

What is Baptism? Is it required for salvation?

Does suffering invalidate God's goodness?

Put this into practice: Make a defense for the message of verse 18.

What makes this passage radical?

Scriptures to Consider:
Matthew 5:38-42
Matthew 5:10-12
Hebrews 9:11-12

# Radical Lifestyle

LESSON 9

# **Radical Lifestyle**
1 Peter 4:1-11  (CSB)

Therefore,[1] since Christ suffered in the flesh, arm yourselves also with the same understanding—because the one who suffers in the flesh is finished with sin[2]— [2] in order to live the remaining time in the flesh no longer for human desires, but for God's will. [3] For there has already been enough time spent in doing what the Gentiles[3] choose to do: carrying on in unrestrained behavior, evil desires, drunkenness, orgies, carousing, and lawless idolatry.[4] [4] They are surprised that you don't join them in the same flood of wild living—and they slander you. [5] They will give an account to the one who stands ready to judge the living and the dead. [6] For this reason the gospel was also preached to those who are now dead,[5] so that, although they might be judged in the flesh according to human standards, they might live in the spirit according to God's standards.

[7] The end of all things is near;[6] therefore, be alert and sober-minded for prayer. [8] Above all, maintain constant love for one another, since **love covers a multitude of sins.** [9] Be hospitable to one another without complaining. [10] Just as each one has received a gift, use it to serve others, as good stewards of the varied grace of God. [11] If anyone speaks, let it be as one who speaks God's words; if anyone serves, let it be from the strength God provides, so that God may be glorified through Jesus Christ in everything. To him be the glory and the power forever and ever. Amen.

---

[1] Peter connects this next section to what has previously been taught, particularly that Christ is victorious over all other powers (Schreiner, 1, 2 Peter, Jude, 199). This knowledge is the hope and encouragement needed to live in the manner prescribed as follows.

[2] Peter is not equating "the one who suffers" to being sinless. Instead, the one who suffers is one who is committed to God no matter the cost. This one is devoted to a new way of living which is noticeably different than their peers or even their former ways (Ibid., 201)

[3] "Pagans of the first century viewed Christians as killjoys who lived gloomy lives devoid of pleasure" (Jobes, 1 Peter, 262). Christians were seen as "haters of humanity and traitors to the Roman way of life" (Ibid., 262).

[4] The listed sins cover unholy practices of sex, food, drink and worship (Ibid., 265). Peter is holistic in his view of holy living.

[5] The "dead" are the Christians who have died. The world assumes their death as proof that their faith was in vain. Peter rightly understands that "death is not the last word for believers. They will be raised from the dead." (Schreiner, 1, 2 Peter, Jude, 208-9).

[6] Biblical writers often use the nearness of the "end of all things" to spur believers to faithful living. This is not a scare tactic or act of deceit because as James puts it "you do not know what tomorrow brings…for you are a mist" (James 4:14).

One Big Thing:

One Confusing Thing:

Is holy living limited living?

How do you balance living holy in an unholy world?

What elements of this world do you still find alluring?

In what ways is the Christian life surprising to the world?

What is meant by Peter's statement "love covers a multitude of sins"?

How can you be hospitable to fellow believers (v. 4:9)?

Verse 10 states that each of us has been given a gift. What do you believe to be your spiritual giftedness? (See 1 Peter 4:11, Romans 12:6-8, 1 Corinthians 12:8-10)

How are you using your gift(s)? Does this point others to Christ?

One Way I Must Respond:

What makes this passage radical?

Scriptures to consider:
Proverbs 10:12
Romans 6:11-14
John 13:34-35

# A Radical Perspective

## LESSON 10

# A Radical Perspective
1 Peter 4:12-19 (ESV)

[12] Beloved, do not be surprised[1] at the fiery trial when it comes upon you to test you, as though something strange were happening to you.[2] [13] But rejoice insofar as you share Christ's sufferings, that you may also rejoice and be glad when his glory is revealed. [14] If you are insulted for the name of Christ, you are blessed, because the Spirit of glory and of God rests upon you.[3] [15] But let none of you suffer as a murderer or a thief or an evildoer or as a meddler.[4] [16] Yet if anyone suffers as a Christian, let him not be ashamed, but let him glorify God in that name. [17] For it is time for judgment to begin at the household of God; and if it begins with us, what will be the outcome for those who do not obey the gospel of God? [18] And

"If the righteous is scarcely saved,

    what will become of the ungodly and the sinner?"[5]

[19] Therefore let those who suffer according to God's will entrust their souls to a faithful Creator[6] while doing good.

One Big Thing:

---

[1] Trials of faith should not be a reason to doubt God (refer back to 1:6-7). Peter uses the word "surprise" in 4:4 and 4:12. Believers must not be surprised but the gentiles should be surprised by how they live in response.

[2] Peter is confident that trials are tests of faith allowed by God to purify the Church. "Sufferings are not a sign of God's absence but his purifying presence" (Schreiner, 1, 2 Peter, Jude, 219).

[3] Experiencing suffering does not equal blessing. The blessing comes from the presence of God (Jobes, 1 Peter, 288).

[4] Peter is clear "Suffering for Christ is a cause for joy, but being mistreated because of one's own sins is nothing to brag about" (Schreiner, 1, 2 Peter, Jude, 220).

[5] See Proverbs 11:31. Peter is making terrifying point that while the suffering upon Christians is horrific and difficult, "how much more will unbelievers suffer for eternity?" (Ibid., 229).

[6] "The reference to God as Creator implies his sovereignty, for the Creator of the world is also sovereign over it." (Ibid., 229).

One Confusing Thing:

Have you ever been surprised by a test or trial? Explain.

What is your natural response to trials?

In Matthew 5:3-9, Jesus offers radical perspective for believers. Which of these stands out to you?

Over the course of your study through 1 Peter, how has your understanding of suffering changed?

Is it ever right to avoid suffering or try to limit it?

How must we practically respond to verses 17-18?

One Way I Must Respond:

What makes this passage radical?

Verses to consider:
James 1:2-4
Matthew 5:10-12
Matthew 10:22

# Closing Remarks

---

LESSON 11

# <u>**Lesson 11 – Closing Remarks**</u>
1 Peter 5:1-14 (ESV)

So[1] I exhort the elders[2] among you, as a fellow elder and a witness of the sufferings of Christ, as well as a partaker in the glory that is going to be revealed: [2] shepherd[3] the flock of God that is among you, exercising oversight, not under compulsion, but willingly, as God would have you; not for shameful gain, but eagerly; [3] not domineering[4] over those in your charge, but being examples to the flock. [4] And when the chief Shepherd appears, you will receive the unfading[5] crown of glory. [5] Likewise, you who are younger,[6] be subject to the elders. Clothe yourselves, all of you, with humility toward one another, for "God opposes the proud but gives grace to the humble."

[6] Humble yourselves, therefore, under the mighty hand of God so that at the proper time he may exalt you, [7] casting all your anxieties on him, because he cares for you. [8] Be sober-minded; be watchful.  Your adversary the devil prowls around like a roaring[7] lion, seeking someone to devour. [9] Resist him, firm in your faith, knowing that the same kinds of suffering are being experienced by your brotherhood throughout the world. [10] And after you have suffered a little while, the God of all grace, who has called you to his eternal glory in Christ, will himself restore, confirm, strengthen, and establish you. [11] To him be the dominion forever and ever. Amen.

[12] By Silvanus, a faithful brother as I regard him, I have written briefly to you, exhorting and declaring that this is the true grace of God. Stand firm in it. [13] She who is at Babylon, who is likewise chosen, sends you greetings, and so does Mark, my son. [14] Greet one another with the kiss[8] of love.

Peace to all of you who are in Christ.

---

[1] A shift is made in this final chapter from the outside suffering imposed by the world/Satan to an internal look at the church as well as each person within it (Schreiner, 1, 2 Peter, Jude, 230-1).

[2] Elders are the spiritual shepherds and leaders of the church and function in similar ways to the modern-day pastor. Peter often writes to elders, as opposed to one elder, as the churches were led by multiple leaders (MacArthur, The MacArthur Bible Commentary, 1920).

[3] The idea of Shepherd as a spiritual leader is used throughout scripture. Jesus is the Good Shepherd (John 10:11). Jesus calls Peter to tend/feed the sheep (John 21:15-19). Now, Peter uses this language for the leaders of the churches all over Asia Minor.

[4] Authority is never an excuse to oppress or abuse power.

[5] Crowns were awarded to victors of competitions or even wars. These prized rewards however do not compare to the "unfading" crown that will be given to the faithful elder of Christ. Recall 1 Peter 1:4 as Peter describes hope in Christ also as "unfading".

[6] Often elders were older members of the congregation, but age did not necessitate position (Jobes, 1 Peter, 307).

[7] "The roar of a lion would scatter a flock of sheep in panic…" (Ibid., 314). Satan's goal is to destroy the church as a body and each Christian individually.

[8] Kissing was a sign of connection and friendship. This practice was especially treasured by "new believers, who were often outcasts from their own families because of their faith (MacArthur, The MacArthur Bible Commentary, 1558).

One Big Thing:

One Confusing Thing:

What are the characteristics of an ungodly leader?

How should we treat the elders in charge of us?

What dangers arise when a congregation lacks humility?

Peter ties together humility and anxiety in the same thought in verses 6-7. How do those relate?

In 5:8, Peter describes the actions of Satan as "prowling like a roaring lion, seeking someone to devour". How does this description shape your view of sin and Satan?

What temptation is being thrown at you this week?

What makes this passage radical?

What is the most impactful piece of 1 Peter that you hope to keep with you?

**As a group read aloud verse 10 and as we close this study, pray over this promise.**

Scriptures to consider:
Luke 4:1-13
James 4:7-8
2 Corinthians 1:3-7

# Bibliography

Jobes, Karen H. *1 Peter*  (Baker Exegetical Commentary on the New Testament; Grand
     Rapids: Baker Academic, 2005).

MacArthur, John. *The MacArthur Bible Commentary* (Nashville: Thomas Nelson, 2005)

Schreiner, Thomas R. *1,2 Peter, Jude*  (The New American Commentary; Nashville:
     Broadman Press, 2003).